In My
Dreams,
I Can Dance

Scripture quotations marked NLT are taken from the *Holy Bible*, New Living Translation, copyright © 1996. Used by permission of Tyndale House Publishers, Inc., Wheaton, Illinois. Scripture quotations marked NIV are taken from the *Holy Bible*, New International Version, copyright © 1973, 1978, 1984 International Bible Society. Used by permission of Zondervan, Grand Rapids, Michigan. Scripture quotations marked NKJV are taken from the New King James Version®. Copyright © 1982 by Thomas Nelson, Inc. Used by permission. All rights reserved. Scripture quotations marked RSV are from the Revised Standard Version, Copyright © OT 1952, NT 1946, Second Edition 1971, Division of Christian Education of the National Council of Churches of Christ in the United States of America. Used by permission. All rights reserved.

Emphasis within scripture quotations is the author's own.

IN MY DREAMS, I CAN DANCE
A Story of Triumph Over Tragedy

ISBN: 978-0-924748-92-9
UPC: 88571300062-8

Printed in the United States of America
© 2008 by Ann Foster

Milestones International Publishers
140 Danika Drive NW
Huntsville, AL 35806
(256) 830-0362; Fax (256) 830-9206
www.milestonesintl.com

Cover design by: Thirty Thumbs Design Works

1 2 3 4 5 6 7 8 9 10 11 / 13 12 11 10 09 08

In My Dreams, I Can Dance

A STORY of TRIUMPH OVER TRAGEDY

ANN FOSTER

MILESTONES
INTERNATIONAL PUBLISHERS

*If I must boast I'd rather boast about
the things that show how weak I am.*
(2 Corinthians 11:30, NLT)

*My gracious favor is all you need. The Holy Spirit said
'My power works best in your weaknesses.' So now I am
glad to boast about my weaknesses, so that the power of
Christ may work through me.*
(2 Corinthians 12:9, NLT)

Endorsements

As we live our busy lives, there are occasionally people that grab our attention. Ann Foster is one of those people. If you need an inspiration, look no further than Ann. She is one of my heroes because she is one of those rare souls that take what life has given her and, without bitterness or anger, has succeeded. Her beautiful family is proof enough that Ann is a winner. Her book, *In My Dreams I Can Dance,* is not only going to be a hit, it is going to set many free from the prison of the question, "Why did this happen to me?" Read it and be changed.

-Mike Hayes, Senior Pastor, Covenant Church of Carrollton

Ann Foster is an example of an overcomer. As she shares her personal testimony of the trials she endured as a child, you will see the hand of God over and over again demonstrated in her life. No matter what you've been through, you will be encouraged as you read her inspiring story of a little girl that the world may have given up on, but by God's grace matures into a mighty woman of God with immovable faith.

-Joni Lamb, Co-Founder of Daystar Television Network

Ann Foster is certainly qualified to write about her subject. Her experiences with pain, rejection, hopelessness, and despair could only be overcome by her encounter with grace and personal relationship with the Lord Jesus. Just recently, I played golf with her husband and she rode along in the golf cart. Had it not been for the crutches, she would have likely been playing with us. Her vibrant personality and overcoming character are on display whether before a congregation or in friendly conversation. I am certain you will be lifted and encouraged by this book.

-Don Dickerman, Author, Evangelist, Friend

Ann is one of those phenomenal personalities who has faced the rain, the storm, and the flood, and yet has maintained an unquenchable fire of passion and devotion for God. When such a person invites you to see what genuine Christianity looks like in everyday life, it's time to pause and give your full attention. In her book, *In My Dreams, I Can Dance,* Ann is throwing a party and it's no time to be a wallflower.

-Pastor Tim Seay, Crossover Church Hyattsville, Maryland

In My Dreams, I Can Dance is a remarkable book about a remarkable woman. The grace with which she handles adversity is matched only by her faith in the goodness of God. She and Carter are one of the great romances of our time and I am sure that this book will move and inspire you.

-Joel A. Brooks, Jr.

Pastor Ann Foster is a powerful woman of God. Her love for the Lord has forged within her strength and trust many have never known. Pastor Ann's story will inspire and encourage anyone who reads it. She is a gift to the body of Christ.

-Ricky Texada, Senior Associate Pastor, Covenant Church

Two thoughts immediately come to my mind ... real world and redemptive. Ann Foster's *In My Dreams, I Can Dance* communicates not from platitude or imagination, but from the real world of Ann's life. Her pain, her struggle, her depth of challenge, flow not from the head but from the heart. You know this story is real, and touches and relates ... deep calls to deep ... those tender places in every life. But not only will you read the agony, Ann's story also tells the ecstasy, the joy of her discovery that our Father always cares for us and works redemptively through every long night through to the joy of the morning. Prepare yourself to relive Ann Foster's real world and experience God's redeeming love to all who call on Him.

-Pastor Eric D. Hulet, Senior Pastor & Teacher, Grace Community Church

Acknowledgments

I want to express my deepest thanks and appreciation to my children, who lived with a handicapped mother without complaint or embarrassment.

Thank you, Dawn, our precious firstborn, who became my legs very early in her life. You would cheerfully go and get whatever I needed – a diaper, pacifier, or book to read as we both cared for David together when he was born. You were only 22 months old then, but you still encouraged me with your sweet, cheerful, and giving spirit. You sing like an angel.

Thank you, David, for bringing so much fun and laughter to me. You were, and are, a friend and leader. Your friends would come to our house to play basketball, swim, eat, or just visit. We affectionately labeled you "the sheriff" since you were a caring and responsible big brother to the younger children.

Debbie, you were always a joy to us. You excelled in everything you did, even graduating as the valedictorian of your class. My thanks go to you for encouraging me. You have been instrumental in opening doors for me to minister. You are a gifted minister who has touched many lives.

My thanks to you, Melanie Faith. You are an evangelist. When you were a small child, you would talk to everyone. You were so unafraid that I was quite concerned. You were, and are, as bold as a lion and you never meet a stranger. You love people and it shows. Even though you lead a very busy life, you took the time to transcribe one of my messages which made putting this book together easier.

Thank you, Daniel, for prodding me to write my story. Thank you for your persistence. An accident cut off your right big toe when you were 22 months old. We received a negative report from the doctor that you would not be able to play basketball, yet we saw you earn a starting spot on the team at four different schools when we moved during your junior and senior high school years. Your strong determination, talent, and love for the Lord have continued to inspire me. You have an overcomer spirit.

My thanks to Freda Dents, whose writing, typing, and computer skills brought everything together for me.

Thank you to the mates that my children have married. Your love for me has been as though God has given me five more children to encourage me to share my story.

To all of you who have come to me after I have spoken and asked, "Do you have a book?" Thank you for wanting to know more.

Finally, thanks to my husband, Carter, whose love for me has been evident for all to see. You are my hero.

Dedication

This book is dedicated to my mother, Jimmie Richie, whom I didn't really know how to appreciate in the depth of her suffering until I became a mother.

I also dedicate it to the love of my life, my husband Carter, who continues to encourage me, love me, and teach me as one who is truly fun to live with.

Table of Contents

Foreword

It is such an honor to write this foreword for my best friend and faithful wife of 47 years. I think that after this length of time I qualify as one who can vouch for her veracity. "My Lady" has faced more pain and difficulties than any ten ladies should have to endure, and yet it has always been embraced with thanksgiving and optimistic faith that all she has walked through will be for building character in her and will also minister life and encouragement to others.

You are in for a real treat as you read this book. My sweetie pie is not only a beautiful lady with a smile that lights up any room she enters, but she also has an inner beauty in her spirit that will shine through the pages as you read them. She radiates the presence of Jesus more intensely not despite what she has endured, but indeed because of the way she has accepted and overcome her struggles.

We met in college, and when I saw her I said what a friend of mine always said, "The Lord is my shepherd, I see what I want." Love at first sight may be a miracle, but for her to still love me after looking at me all these years is an even greater miracle. She has an ability to impart faith. Many times, I wondered how we could make it, but she never wavered. She had faith for me when my well was dry.

This same miracle will happen as you read these pages. Faith and encouragement will be imparted to you. It is with joy that I invite you to read on and learn from one of the most optimistic and encouraging people I know. She is my wife, mother of my five children, grandmother of sixteen, and a living story that will touch your spirit. Open your heart and dream with her and you will come away dancing.

Carter Foster
June 2008

Introduction

The severe and obvious disability of my body is the first thing that people may notice about me, but I pray that if you take a second and closer look, you will see someone with a message of hope and encouragement. Somehow I know that the message of my life can bring freedom to those who think we are limited by our pains, physically or emotionally, or by the obstacles that seem to hold us captive. I am a survivor of polio. I was four years old when this disease ravaged my body and most of my childhood was spent in and out of hospitals having corrective surgery.

Polio left me severely crippled in both legs and burdened with a curve in my spine. My story shares how, for over 50 years, I have learned to function normally in life, borne and raised five children, and pursued my purpose of serving God while walking with crutches and braces.

My story is one that shows God's faithfulness and His grace in demonstrating His strength through my weakness. He has shown me how to do the impossible with His help. My story demonstrates His love for me by giving me a strong, handsome, and godly husband. God has helped me by placing a song in my heart and in my mouth that enables me to praise my way through pain and difficulties while strengthening my polio-weakened lungs.

My journey had led me through the valley of the shadow of death, where I have come face-to-face with evil spirits. God has taught me how to find and walk in deliverance and healing so I can show others the way out by way of the Cross of Jesus.

As I lay bare my soul in these pages, I pray that the Lord will inspire, encourage, strengthen, and correct by the power of the Holy Spirit making Himself real to you.

Chapter One
Younger Years

In the beginning, there was pain. The pain was greater than my ability to describe it. In 1945, there were not many safe drugs available to administer to a small four-year-old child. However, a woman named Sister Kinney devised a plan to ease the pain by wrapping warm blankets around those areas that hurt the most. My entire body was swathed in hot, damp, wool blankets which allowed me some relief and blessed sleep.

From my early childhood days, I have felt and known the grace and mercy of the Lord

From my early childhood days, I have felt and known the grace and mercy of the Lord in my life. My parents were Christians and they taught me not the just song, but the reality that "Jesus Loves Me." On May 28, 1945, when I was four years old, I became ill with what appeared to be the flu. Yet as time progressed, my condition worsened and my fever increased. When the high fever subsided and it was determined finally that I had a chance to survive, they tried to assess the damage to my body. I was taken to the quarantine section of Grady Hospital in Atlanta, Georgia. This was to begin the first of what was to be many long weeks of separation from my parents. The diagnosis was polio. For three weeks, the disease did its damage to my muscles and nerves.

Poliomyelitis, commonly known as polio, is a highly infectious disease that damages nerves and can cause paralysis. It is caused by a virus and transmitted via water contaminated with fecal material. The virus enters the body through the mouth, multiplies in the intestines, and then migrates to the central nervous system. It destroys spinal cord cells that are the starting point for nerves governing movement. The very word polio still sparks fear and dread. Even still, new cases in the United States are rare because of the discovery of a vaccine.

When my mother left me there in the emergency room to fill out the paperwork, she could hear me crying. She wanted to come to me, but was told, "You cannot go to her again, Mrs. Coleman." She replied, "Well, I'm going anyway." She was informed that she would be arrested, because this was a communicable disease. At that point, I was not allowed to see her again for three weeks, and when some stranger came to my bedside, it was to "hurt" me. The confusion and fear I felt, along with the perception that I had been abandoned and rejected, produced in me an emotional pain as great as the torment my body was enduring. Just months earlier, my daddy had been drafted into the Marines. I was a "Daddy's girl" and still could not understand why he was gone. Not yet over the trauma of that separation, I was now even without my mother's comfort.

When my fever began to subside, paralysis remained. For three weeks, I did not speak at all. My mother says I had cried so long, for so hard, that I may have had a sore throat. There was also the probability of brain damage. The first words I spoke when a nurse handed me an ice cream cone were "Thank you." Mother said she could hear the nurse screaming all the way down the hall. *"She said thank you!"* she yelled. Both of my legs and my back were completely paralyzed. My bed was by a window where I was propped up on a pillow. I could raise my head just a little to see my mother and grandparents sitting outside by a tree.

Although he was not permanently discharged, my daddy was granted a furlough to come home when I went into the hospital. He told the story of how someone had to volunteer to take his place in order for him to be released. Some caring Marine gave his life for my family, because that unit was later left with no survivors when they landed in the war zone.

I was transferred from Grady Hospital in Atlanta to Warm Springs, Georgia. It was a hospital made famous by President Roosevelt, who had also suffered from polio. The warm spring water, for which the town was named, soothed the intense pain and made recovery from surgery easier.

One of the worst things for me was the forced separation from my family. Since my parents did not have a car, it would have been very difficult for them to visit me every day, even if the hospital authorities had allowed it. They had to ride the bus almost 60 miles from Atlanta and could only see me for a few hours on Sundays. Visiting hours were very strict because a visit from parents created crying children when they left. I was a very lonely and frightened little girl. Before polio, I was a happy, outgoing child with high energy, always running or skipping. My parents assured and comforted me with the words that Jesus would always be there with me. That is when I began to talk with Him as my friend. In my loneliness, I drew closer to Him.

After months of lying immobile in a hospital bed, it would take more painful months of learning to walk again after each operation. I spent most of my childhood in and out of the hospital. I can count ten incisions on my legs, plus the pinholes through each knee. The surgery was intended to correct the deformity of my crooked body. Both of my feet were twisted so that I could only stand on the sides of them and my kneecaps met one another face to face. My spine was also twisted very badly. On three different occasions, I had to be put in a complete body cast. How I hated it! I was encased from my underarms downward.

I spent most of my childhood in and out of the hospital.

The climate in Georgia is really hot in the summertime and there was no air conditioning. Underneath my body cast was a layer of thick cotton, and this cotton would become soaked with perspiration. Then the itching would start. It was like torture to me. When the cast was cut off my body, the doctors' would find objects like pencils, rulers, and whatever else I could find available to scratch with. First, I would pull the cotton out of the top of my cast so I could scratch. Most of the time, I would lose my hold on the objects and be forced to lie on them until the cast was replaced.

Surgery was performed on my left hip to correct back deformity. My left leg would be stretched while I was in the body cast and pulled around so that I would view my left foot over my right shoulder. When the pain became too great, they would stop the stretching and cast me that way. I never received pain medication. The first surgery was not successful and the process had to be repeated. After the second surgery, I was released for a visit to go home.

I was so excited about going home. Yeah! I remember being in my grandparents' backyard, where I reached up to a low-hanging limb on a small tree and fell, breaking my fragile right leg. The long recovery from the broken leg kept me sitting in a wheelchair, which undid all that the former surgeries had accomplished. I had to go back into the hospital and be put into another body cast.

While I was at Warm Springs, along with the physical and emotional pain, three major things happened. The first, and best, was when my parents brought me a little record player and records. I learned to sing along with the records, shortly after my voice was restored, while lying flat on my back following the three weeks of silence. This gift of song was planted as a seed of praise and thankfulness which God has used to keep me from the bitterness and despair which would try to buffet me through the years to come. Singing was a good way for me to exercise my polio-weakened lungs. It became a way for me to face my fears and the shame of my deformed appearance. I had no way of knowing how far-reaching it would become in my life. Singing defined my life choices when I went to college on a music scholarship majoring in voice. A song helped me catch the attention of my yet-to-be husband Carter, when he heard me.

Singing became a way for me to face my fears.

The second event occurred when I was placed in a dark room at the hospital for being "bad". How bad can a four-year-old in a body cast be? The "dark room" was a windowless interior room where the stretchers and wheelchairs were stored. I was alone and it was very dark and hot. It was there that I met the spirit of fear face-to-face. Fighting fear would impact my life for many years to come.

The third life shaping event was learning how to read. Since I was a bedridden child, I read all the time. Because I read so voraciously, I was able to pass all the tests required for each grade level. I only attended school for three months when I was in the fourth grade. Other years, we had the surgeries at the beginning of the summer so that I would not miss all of the school year by being in the hospital.

One other major event happened at the hospital in Warm Springs. I think I must have been about ten or eleven years old. I was in the therapy and recovery stage of a surgery and had progressed to a wheelchair. There were no televisions available in the hospital, but once or twice a week a movie would be shown in the adjoining building for those who were ambulatory enough to attend.

The orderlies were assigned to push us over. I was so excited to be attending the movie that I had already mentally marked out for myself the exact spot where I wanted to sit in front of the screen. I was boxed in on both sides by those in wheelchairs to my side and those in stretchers behind me. One of the male orderlies sat right in front of me and I spent the entire time fighting him off as he tried to touch me in an inappropriate manner. I remembered the punishment that I received for crying out or screaming and did not want to spend more time in the "dark room", thus I kept quiet.

After the movie was over, I began to tell my friends what had happened and a nurse overheard me and she took some action. The results were that my parents came to get me. They chose not to press charges, to spare me a court appearance. After that, I never had to go back to Warm Springs.

Doctors recommended more surgery, but the last one I had took place in Atlanta when I was twelve years old. It allowed me to successfully remove the braces from my right leg and back. I pleaded for a break from surgeries after that to give me some normal time for going to school with my friends.

Chapter Two

Growing Pains

Some of you might remember the television series called *Growing Pains*. The program featured a dad who was a psychologist and a mom who was a journalist. They had four kids who gave them various challenges, or growing pains. Despite occasional problems, they still remained close. To a degree, I guess this could describe my own family. I'm sure I gave my parents more than their share of growing pains.

When I was nine years old, during a revival meeting, I made a public confession of Jesus as Lord and was water baptized.

My brother George was born when I was ten years old. I loved him so much. I was so proud to get to hold him. We had normal sibling rivalry, but my brother and I are close friends now and the sweet young man has become a wonderful Christian husband and father, as well as a caring son to our sweet mother, who is now widowed.

As I grew older, I wanted to try all the things that everybody else did to be normal. I grew up as a good little Christian girl. I was trying to do what the Bible told me to do. It said to be obedient, and since I loved God, I wanted to please Him.

As I grew older, I wanted to try all the things that everybody else did.

I was constantly doing something that I should not have been doing. After each incident, I would rededicate my life to God. I was always at the front of the church and became a chronic rededicator. I thought, *I just can't live like God wants me to live.* This was a time of spiritual growing pains for me. In fact, the accuser was always reminding me of how bad I was.

As a teenager, I did all sorts of rebellious things. I would sneak out to meet my boyfriends, and once I convinced one of them to take me horseback riding. My parents had said I could not go, but because I had read all the *Black Stallion* books, as well as others on horsemanship, I thought that I knew everything I needed to know about riding horses. The result was that I was thrown off into a fence, from a full gallop, when my horse stepped into a hole. The impact broke a blood vessel in my left hand and I had to call my parents from the doctor's office. I almost always got caught in my wild antics.

As I shared, I would sing when I was in the hospital. During those days, there was not much known about therapy for the lungs. However, God knew and He gave me a voice to sing to Him. Singing kept my lungs working well. I would sit in my wheelchair on my grandmother's front porch and I sing in my "foreign language". I called it opera and Jesus was my audience. I would say, "Okay, Jesus, I'm going to sing this to You." I would sing at the top of my lungs. I had decided that I would become an opera star.

During my teen years, singing brought me some wonderful opportunities. It was my job. I got paid to sing at weddings, and there were lots of fun parties, too. I also auditioned and was the guest soloist with the Atlanta Pops Orchestra's summer series. I sang with the Atlanta Symphony Chorus and learned the soprano solos in Handel's Messiah, which I was also able to sing in other places as life progressed. Through a school music director, I was able to audition with and study voice under a renowned Metropolitan Opera Star. My goal became to sing with the Metropolitan.

When I was sixteen, I was down at the front of the church, rededicating my life again. I had a heart tender toward the Lord, but I needed a lot of reassurance. Therefore, I was very insecure, so I went looking for affirmation in all the wrong places. The Lord would convict me of my sins because I was guilty of exploiting young men's emotions. I gave up my dream of being an opera star when I gave my life completely to the Lord and felt a call into the ministry.

In reading the Bible, I found two verses in Matthew that really caught my attention. *"I tell you the truth, if you have faith as small as a mustard seed, you can say to this mountain, 'Move from here to there' and it will move. Nothing will be impossible for you"* (Matthew 17:20, NIV) *Again, I tell you that if two of you on earth agree about anything you ask for, it will be done for you by my Father in heaven. For where two or three come together in my name, there am I with them* (Matthew 18:19-20, NIV).

I tried to have the faith required for healing my body, but often I could not separate faith from hope or from just wishing or dreaming. My faith would often waver and I would say with the Apostle Paul, "The things I don't want to do are the very things I do." I would doubt my salvation and wonder if I had really been born again.

Through all of these growing pains, letting go of becoming an opera singer, stopping the downward spiral of exploiting other peoples' emotions, I decided to attend Shorter College in Rome, Georgia. There, I received a full music scholarship in voice and planned to become a full-time church musician.

When Carter Foster attended a senior weekend at Shorter College, he stood with a group of other students to listen to me sing. I was auditioning for my scholarship. He was introduced to me along with several others but, I am embarrassed to admit, I did not remember him.

When he was elected president of the freshman class the following year, I of course knew who he was. He had a car, and I did not, so I asked for a ride to church one Sunday night in October. From that point on, we saw one another daily and became engaged at Christmas. Everyone was opposed. My dad, who had carried me in his arms when I was a child any time stairs were involved, became ill at the thought that I would marry so young and unprepared.

One after another, the very good reasons for not getting married accumulated.

I would lose my parents' health insurance coverage by getting married. We had seven more years of school to complete (college and graduate school). Carter was only 18 years old and did not have a well-paying job. One after another, the very good reasons for not getting married accumulated. However, we were very much in love and determined to prove to everyone that it was the right thing for us.

We were married the following June. Carter was working as a car salesman. We also had a church job as Ministers of Music at a small church outside of Rome, Georgia. In October, Carter preached at a conference where a church search committee heard him. As a result, he became the full-time pastor of Everett Springs Baptist Church in the rural town of Everett Springs, Georgia.

Chapter Three

Children, Are You Kidding?

Behold, children are a gift of the LORD.
The fruit of the womb is a reward - Psalms 127:3

"How did you manage to have and take care of five children?"

The question the young mother asked me was referring to the fact that I can only walk with the help of two crutches and a heavy brace on my left leg. Indeed, because of my physical disability, no one thought that I could become pregnant. Our plan was to complete three more years of college and four years of graduate school before we would try to have children. We discovered three different methods of birth control that did not work for us. Four of our children were unplanned, but certainly not unwanted. We view each of them as a precious gift from God.

I remember looking anxiously out of the window of the big jet trying to see this strange new city that was to be my home. Carter had graduated from college on Sunday afternoon and then driven all night the 500 unfamiliar miles to enroll in summer school at the Southern Baptist Seminary in Louisville, Kentucky on Monday morning.

Now, a week later, I was flying to join him. In the past 22 months, I had had two babies and major abdominal surgery. That fact, in addition to caring for my three-week-old baby, had prompted my parents to make sure that I did not make the trip by car. This time we listened to them, as so often in the past we had not.

Our impetuous young love had not been able to see why we should not marry with yet another seven years of school looming before us. Getting married meant no more health insurance. My dad had carried me on his Georgia Power Company insurance. Because of my preexisting condition, I was uninsurable except under a group policy. Our medical expenses now became out of pocket expenses for us.

We lived in the beautiful rural community of Everett Springs, 30 miles outside of Rome where we attended Shorter College.

When I became pregnant, shortly after we were married, my education changed from music to motherhood. In fact, I only recently completed all my education in January 2006, when all of our children were grown and out on their own. I received my Doctorate in Philosophy with an emphasis in Theology.

With my first pregnancy, I developed toxemia and other complications. We considered it a miracle that I delivered a healthy, beautiful little girl. We named her Dawn.

Caring for her after her arrival proved to be a greater challenge than the pregnancy had been, because I use my arms to walk with my crutches. I relied on a stroller or carriage to carry her when necessary, but mostly I held and rocked her.

When I went back to the doctor for my six-week check-up, he found a cyst on my right ovary the size of a grapefruit. I had major abdominal surgery when Dawn was five months old. As soon as I weaned Dawn, I became pregnant with David. Again toxemia set in, however David was born, three weeks premature, an otherwise healthy baby, but a little jaundiced. At this time, Dawn was only 22 months old.

Despite the lack of insurance with two complicated pregnancies and a major surgery added to our college tuition, God miraculously enabled us to leave Georgia debt-free. On paper, it was impossible, but God supernaturally provided for us. We always tithed. God is faithful to us when we are faithful to Him.

The Louisville, Kentucky that I met consisted of Seminary Village, the housing provided for married couples with children, and an occasional trip to the grocery store. We were a family of four but did not qualify for a two-bedroom apartment. In order to get two bedrooms, there had to be three children. We decided to put our children in the bedroom. Carter and I slept on an old hide-a-bed in the living room. It was a tiny place in the middle of the old apartment building.

We shared our entrance with three other families. With most of the wives working to help put their husbands through school, I found it to be a very, very lonely place. I was unable to go out and meet people because of my needing to rely on the stroller or Carter's help to carry my babies from place to place, even in the apartment. When they learned to walk, and they were all early walkers, it was both a blessing and a greater challenge to keep up with them.

The children and I spent our days washing diapers. It was a long, tiring process. I would rinse them in the commode, put them into the diaper pail, squeeze the water from each one, and place them into the washing machine. We did not own a dryer, which made the laundry ordeal an even bigger task. I had to hang them outside on clotheslines. The lines were located behind the building and our apartment did not have a back door.

I would bundle up my two children, put David into the stroller to push him around the building to the back, then retrieve the wet clothes from the open window where I had placed them. I would drag the basket over to the clothesline, where I would hang them using only one hand. My other arm always had my crutch to help me keep my balance.

There was great rejoicing at our house when we finally got a dryer after our third child, Debbie, was born. There were even more hallelujahs after our fourth child, Melanie, was born because someone in our church was able to get disposable diapers for us. It was great knowing that I could actually throw them away!

Carter offered what help he could, but my fresh young college graduate was working each day after school for the seminary, doing things like cutting grass and painting the gutters of those steep old roofs. After a thirty minute break for dinner, he went to work on campus, running the switchboard until 10:00 at night. Then he would drag himself wearily home to study for the next day's classes. On weekends, we drove all over Kentucky and southern Indiana, supplying relief for vacationing pastors. The little money that it brought in helped, of course, but the opportunity to preach was the motivating factor. I was often too sick to accompany him.

My body had not yet recovered from the onslaught of the past two years. I was nursing a baby, had two in diapers, and the small apartment was very old. In fact, disease lurked in the very walls. When the first snow storm hit in October, I developed a fever, which was followed by pneumonia symptoms. I did not get a formal diagnosis because I did not have a chest x-ray. However, God provided a wonderful doctor friend, so we did not have to deal with medical bills. He played an important part in our lives on several levels.

Dr. Bob and his wife Joan were also studying at the seminary, preparing to go to Nigeria as medical missionaries. We met them in the fall when school started. Joan and I were both in the choir at the Crescent Hills Baptist Church. While waiting for us one evening, Carter and Bob became acquainted. This led to Bob giving Carter his school physical. We soon learned that they lived across the street from us and were, just like us, very hungry to know more about God.

We had all quickly discovered that the seminary could not provide the devotional life we sought, so the four of us began a weekly prayer time together. Another couple, Ken and Jackie, soon joined us. Ken was a pharmacist who was also planning on going to the mission field. I was thrilled to finally have some friends.

When I became sick, Dr. Bob gave me penicillin shots twice a day and did all he could to help me. He finally told us that what I needed was a hospital stay, or bed rest to recover. To us, that seemed impossible, because I had to do diapers and take care of my children, and we had no insurance. We did what we felt would be the best and most logical choice: the children and I went home to Atlanta to stay with my parents, where I was able to get a lot of tender loving care and see a local doctor.

We ended up staying for nine weeks. I was fully rested, but my lung condition did not improve and I continued to go downhill physically. The doctors in Atlanta seemed as baffled as those in Louisville. I became incredibly lonely for Carter, and he missed us also, so we went back to Kentucky. At that time, I was taking 22 pills per day in order to combat the lung infection. I knew I was dying, so I began planning for my death.

During my nine week visit to Atlanta to heal, Carter had gotten a job as a librarian after school. He had a student assistant, which made studying a little easier for him. While working at the library, David Wilkerson's book, *The Cross and The Switchblade*, came across his desk. He read the first chapter and then brought it home to share with me. I would read it out loud on the weekends when we were doing our weekly two-hour travel to Vine Run, Kentucky to pastor a church.

The church there provided a nice house for us. I was happy to stay there while Carter was off visiting with the parishioners. After settling the children into bed, I continued to pray and seek God about what I had been reading. David Wilkerson's account of his father's healing had moved and spoken to me deeply. When Carter arrived home that day, I said to him, "If I'm going to die, I'm going to do so trusting in God to heal me. I'm not taking any more of this medicine. I know that I heard God tell me what to do." This was our introduction to the healing of the Holy Spirit when He touched me in a new and powerful way.

Within three weeks, I was totally healed and restored. Praise God! I have since taken lots of medicine and been under a doctor's care. I never want to presume that what God says to do on one occasion means the same for all the others. We must walk by constantly listening and being obedient to His voice.

After my healing, I became pregnant again. Debbie was born when David was 22 months old. This time I had a healthy pregnancy, with no signs of toxemia or any other health issues. When God touched me and filled me with His Spirit, I was changed both physically and emotionally. This experience opened up for me a whole new understanding of the supernatural.

Since I was a reader, the first change that I noticed was that the Word of God had become real, fresh, and new to me, even though I had read it through many times before. I began to devour it. I saw things I had never seen so clearly before. My experience had proven to me that God does still heal miraculously and my hope was fueled for a miracle in my legs. It also began the process of setting me free from the fear that had tormented me since childhood.

Carter also had a life-changing experience with the Holy Spirit and we were both eager to share with everyone about my healing and what had happened to us. Within two months, we had led over 200 people into an encounter with the Holy Spirit and small prayer groups began to spring up around the city. This laid the groundwork for what was to become New Covenant Christians and The Jesus People Movement in Louisville, Kentucky.

After Debbie was born, we became eligible for a two-bedroom apartment in Seminary Village. However, the two bedrooms and one bath were upstairs with a small living area and kitchen downstairs. This meant finding creative ways to get my baby upstairs (the two toddlers could walk by now) when we needed to go. I sat down and scooted on my bottom, holding her in one arm. As I look at more recent inventions, like slings and backpacks for babies, I think about how much easier it would have been if they had been available to me.

After seminary, we moved to Tell City, Indiana to pastor a church there. When Debbie was four years old, we were surprised by the birth of yet another wonderful little girl, Melanie Faith. I am sure people had lots of questions, but they were too polite to ask. That didn't stop them from staring at me – crippled, pregnant, with three small children already. Melanie was only 18 months old when Daniel came along to complete our family. I was 30 years old and now had five beautiful, healthy children.

We moved back to Louisville when Melanie was a baby. We enjoyed nine more wonderful years pastoring and raising our family there. After Louisville, we moved to San Antonio to begin a new church. There were different kinds of challenges there, but now that all the kids could walk and dress themselves, my handicap became a more manageable problem.

Chapter Four

Being Content in All Circumstances

Christmas is my favorite time of year. It is a season of joy, thankfulness, and the expressing of love. From my childhood, I was taught that the giving of gifts to one another was a way of expressing our love to Jesus. We, the church, are His body, and in John 13:34, Jesus gives us a commandment to love one another. Just as He loves us, we are to love one another. Then He goes on to say, *By this all men will know that you are my disciples, if you love one another* (John 13:35, NIV). To me, giving or receiving a gift is just another way to say "I love you."

45

One day, while seeking the Lord about what we should give to whom, He reminded me of His Christmas present to me in 1971. He has given me many gifts, materially, physically and spiritually, before and after this particular one. Yet, as I reflected on His goodness, praise and wonderment flooded me afresh.

The prayer group had been in total unity when they agreed that Carter should leave the church in Tell City, Indiana and move back to Louisville as their full-time pastor. Up until then, we had been driving the 100 miles every Wednesday to meet with a handful of eager, Spirit-filled Christians. There was great joy and excitement about these trips – the kind you feel when you know you are where God wants you to be. We never minded the two-hour drive after midnight, usually finding it a good time to pray and be together. I was pregnant with Melanie during most of this period, however, and I would frequently fall asleep. I laughed as I remembered waking up to find Carter with his head out the window in the cold night air, singing at the top of his lungs, trying to stay awake.

In July 1970, we loaded all of our earthly goods into a few cars and the back of a pick-up truck and moved into a house we had rented for our newly established church building. We lived on the main level and the church, now known as New Covenant Christians, met in the basement. The upstairs was rented out. In our Indiana church, we had lived in a furnished trailer. Besides the baby bed for our new little Melanie, we had only a piano, table, two lamps, and a rocker. God began to bless us through His people as they shared what they could with us.

The rent was high and the number of people was small. The way our finances were handled, out of necessity, came to be that all the bills were paid and the pastor received whatever was left. For the first six months, the leftover averaged $56.00 a week.

While in Indiana, I had worked for a cosmetic company on a commission basis and God had blessed me. After moving to Louisville, I attempted to continue working, but having a small baby and not having been in town long enough to have many contacts made it a constant struggle. In the year I had worked, with God's blessing, I had climbed right up the success ladder. In building a business, I had put most of my profit back into buying product, so now I found myself in a position to begin making money and God said, "Now quit." It seemed unreasonable in light of the $56.00 a week salary, but as I look back on it, I am so glad I quit in obedience to Him. Just two months later, in February, God began to pour people into our lives and we became known as the Jesus people. We also discovered we were going to have another baby, which meant I would not have had time to work anyway.

In the midst of all this, the Lord gave us a wonderful Christmas present – a new house. It was not just any old house, it was the one He chose just for us, I believe. Through a word of prophecy, He told us to begin looking for a house that would meet our needs. We looked, but nothing seemed just right for us. Finally, one day our realtor friend came by and half-jokingly commented that he could show us a nice house with a swimming pool, since we had decided to look at three-bedroom homes.

We felt good about it from the moment we walked in the front door. It was almost love at first sight. We went from top to bottom, saying oohs and aahs. It probably would not have been so beautiful to anyone else, but the Lord had prepared our hearts to receive with love His gift to us. It included three flights of stairs, but I knew God would show me how to manage them. The pool was a wonderful bonus. Swimming is the only exercise I am really able to enjoy. Hallelujah, Jesus is so personal, so loving, and so caring.

Carter turned to me as we were walking down the stairs from the bedrooms and said, "Well, I have eleven cents and that is the total amount of our savings in the bank account." We knew in our hearts that God had led us this far and that we were now to wait upon Him for further direction. In the next four weeks, I must confess, we tried to figure out how the Lord was going to perform His miracle of finances, with dead-end results.

Then came a surprise. One day, a friend came by and casually handed Carter an envelope. Thinking it to be a letter from one of the friend's children in college, he opened it and sat in stunned silence as a check for $3,000 stared up at him. Praise God for answered prayer and for people who become His instruments. Here was our down payment.

Over the course of the four weeks prior to that, there had been four bids placed on the house. We had never met the owners, only the realtor in charge, but God had worked so that all four bids were turned down and we were free to place ours. It was accepted. Then the second miracle happened: our loan was accepted. Can you imagine the disbelief on the part of the man who wrote our application as he asked the questions? For instance, "How long have you been a Kentucky resident?" Answer: "Three months." Then, "How much is your salary per week?" Answer: "Well, it varies from week to week, but averages $56.00." Here we were, promising by faith to make house payments that amounted to more per month than our total salary. God worked a miracle in someone's heart or blinded some businessman's eyes. However, He did it, and we gave Him praise.

We moved in just in time for Christmas. Carter's mother came and bought us a refrigerator for a Christmas present. There came a time that winter when we left the house locked, with an empty refrigerator, and returned home to find food in it, miraculously. We felt like the children of Israel whose shoes did not wear out and were fed from heaven.

In December and January, our membership did not increase, but, miracle number three, our salary did. We had just enough to pay our bills.

This Christmas present from Jesus signified much more to me than the house itself. I must bare my heart and tell you how much God had to break out of me before He could bless us with a nice home. When I was just a little girl, I would talk to my friend, Jesus. I would ask Him for things and tell Him just what I wanted. I did not realize the painful process it would take to get me ready to receive God's blessings without ruining me with pride or taking them lightly. You see, He wanted my heart, my fellowship, and my willingness to do His will more than He wanted to bless me with things. I know very well that I must hold these blessings with an open hand, never grasping.

When we first married, I said to Carter, "Honey, I love you so much. I would live in a tree-hut with you." There were times I longed for a private little tree-hut in the ensuing years. We moved into a 28-foot trailer our first year, and from there to an old farm house where you could see light between the cracks in the walls. Dawn and David were born there.

We lived in places where I battled dirt and roaches. The greatest battle took place in my soul as I longed to have a house I could decorate and be comfortable in. I wanted pretty furniture and, oh, how I coveted a dryer or a dishwasher or an air-conditioner. My list grew endless as we struggled to stretch the grocery money. I thought, "If we just get through school, things will get better."

The transformation inside me had been slow in coming. We faced hardships, but they were all used to teach me to say with Paul, "I have learned, in whatever state I am, to be content." As time moved on, I realized that it could well have been God's will for us to spend the rest of our lives in that small town, in that small trailer, as nobodies who had done nothing of particular significance in the world's eyes. Even so, we could have been of eternal value to His kingdom.

I can now look back on this time as a necessary wilderness, growing, breaking, learning, and yielding experience. Then, at long last, I learned to regard it as a paradise, a time when from my heart I could say to Carter, "Honey, when I felt God's call for something special when I was younger, I know now it was not to make my mark in the music world, but to be your wife – to be your helper and the mother of your children and to be content to spend the rest of my life right here or wherever you are."

One day, while sitting by the pool watching my children at play, the Lord spoke to me. He said, "Ann, do you remember when we talked when you were a little child and you asked Me for a two-story house with a swimming pool? You said you wanted five children, you wanted a horse and a collie, and a tall, dark, handsome preacher husband, and for Me to heal your legs." I bowed my head and wept with gratitude. Because He had answered every prayer but the one to heal my legs – my faith in Him grew as I waited eagerly for that prayer to be answered as well.

Photo Album

Ann standing in the middle before Polio at about 2 years of age.

Me and my dad at Warm Springs.

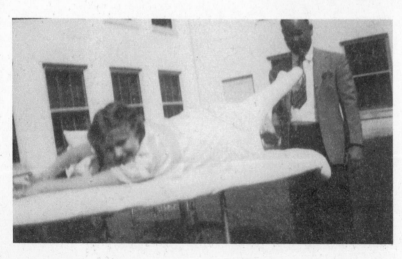

In a body cast with my daddy holding my legs on a visit.

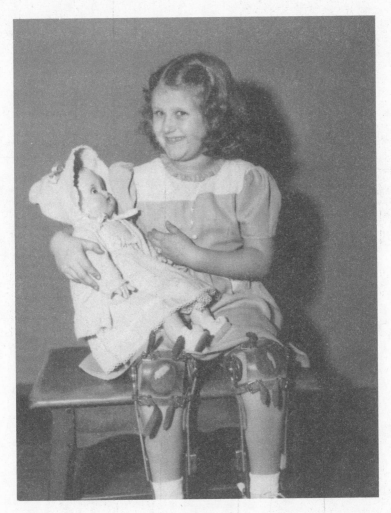

Ann at 5 years old.

BEVERLY ANN A BOOSTER

Atlanta School Children Support March of Dimes

School children in the Atlanta area are aiding the March of Dimes drive—but no special appeals will be needed in schools like Central Park in East Point where 11-year-old Beverly Ann Coleman is proof positive of the campaign's value.

Dimpled, blue-eyed Beverly Ann has received March of Dimes assistance since that bright May day seven years ago when she first was stricken with polio.

"Today, she's one of our best pupils!" attests her teacher, Mrs. W. H. Hembree.

Although she must wear leg braces and use crutches to walk, Beverly Ann joins her classmates on the playground in playing baseball, kick ball and other games.

"She's a wonderful little sport," her teacher points out.

In past years, Beverly Ann has told other school children about the March of Dimes and how it helped her. She probably will do the same to aid the current drive which will continue through Jan. 31.

Beverly Ann's parents, Mr. and Mrs. G. R. Coleman, of 414 Jones St., East Point, are equally grateful for the funds provided by the Georgia Chapter, National Foundation for Infantile Paralysis.

HORRIBLE NIGHTMARE

"When I learned Beverly Ann had polio," her mother said, "it was like a nightmare. It seemed the worst thing possible. My husband was in service, and the only income I had was his $80 allotment."

Mrs. Coleman was admittedly "relieved" when she learned the March of Dimes would help her polio-stricken child.

Beverly Ann spent a month at Grady Hospital and nine months at the Warm Springs Foundation. She had a severe case of polio. Her back and left shoulder as well as her legs were involved.

She has undergone four operations to straighten her back and right leg, and she still must go to the Warm Springs Foundation for a checkup every three months. Her mother gives her physical therapy at home.

"I feel fine now," she grins happily.

Beverly Ann is studying music —and her ambition is to become an opera singer.

SCHOOLS PARTICIPATE

The March of Dimes and the Junior Red Cross drive are the only two campaigns permitted in Atlanta schools. But school officials consider the fight against polio so important they allow collection boxes to be placed in the school buildings.

Miss Ira Jarrell, Atlanta school superintendent, is school chairman of the March of Dimes.

She pointed out there were a few children, who have had polio, in nearly every school. Pupils learn about polio not only from the polio victims themselves but in health and science classes where polio research is discussed.

Atlanta's school radio station, WABE-FM, will have programs promoting the March of Dimes and the war against polio throughout January.

Goal of the polio campaign in Fulton and DeKalb Counties is $200,000. Minimum goal for Georgia is $806,000. Contributions should be sent to the March of Dimes headquarters, 41 Exchange Pl., S. E.

POLIO VICTIM AIDS MARCH OF DIMES DRIVE
Beverly Ann Coleman smiles at teacher, Mrs. W. H. Hembree.

A 1952 Newspaper story featuring Ann and her participation in the March of Dimes.

At Warm Springs at 10 or 11 years old.

Ann at the age of 8 or 9 years old.

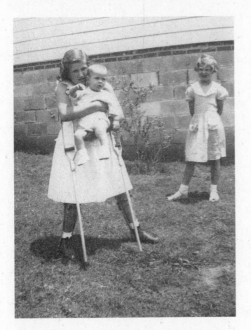

Ann at 11 years old holding my brother, George. My Cousin Patsy watching afraid I would drop him.

We were married June 18, 1961

*In College Carter took this
right after we met.*

*Ann, in the Den after the
broken knee.*

Singing on a Cruise ship October 2006

Chapter Five

In the Midst of the Mess

Messes (a dirty, untidy, or disordered condition) seem to be synonymous with children. They know how to mix things up and scatter them all over the floor and have a great time doing so. It tends to bother us adults because most of the time we will be the ones doing the clean up.

Our youngest son, Daniel, had just turned three years old. I was sitting on the floor playing with him and his new putt-putt train. I began thinking of how he has been God's instrument in my life. Each of my children has brought their own special blessing, and I praise God that they are all unique individuals to be loved for who they are. Yet Daniel has been the one who has caused me to eat every word I ever said about raising children. He entered the world as a child of life and laughter, curiosity and charm, and a bundle of strength and energy.

He began to walk at not quite eight months and, from that point on, he could not be contained. At twelve months old, he no longer slept in a baby bed because he kept climbing out. I would find him sitting on my dresser applying make-up or in the bathroom pouring shampoo down the drain. I remember how frustrated I was. At one point in particular, when I just could not seem to get ahead, always trying to keep him from getting hurt while cleaning up endless messes, I cried out to God. I felt so sorry for myself, so helpless and frustrated. I had been trusting God as best as I could to heal my legs. I remember saying to Him, almost in anger, "God, I need help now! If you are ever going to restore my legs so I can throw away these crutches and brace, now is the time! And if you are not going to heal me, why don't you do something? You saw him make that mess."

God was doing something, something in my spirit that I could not yet recognize. Then, about a year later, He was gracious enough to show me some of what He had done. Daniel, Melanie, and I were in the basement doing the laundry and Daniel decided to go upstairs. I finished loading the washer and, as I climbed the stairs, I heard him in the kitchen making those sounds that I recognized as trouble. He heard me coming also and quickly took off up the stairs.

About a dozen eggs had been broken on the kitchen floor. The gooey mess was creeping under the refrigerator and scattered about among the egg shells were assorted items from the refrigerator, such as a bottle of ketchup, mayonnaise, and jelly. My eyes took in at a glance what he had done and I followed his dripping trail over the carpet, up the stairs, and to the bathroom where I found him trying to take off his sticky, wet clothes.

No matter how they behave, mothers always manage to find excuses for their children, like, "He is just tired, sweet little darling." I am convicted by Proverbs 20:11, *Even a child makes himself known by his deed, whether what he does is pure and right* (NKJV), and Proverbs 22:15, *Folly is bound up in the heart of a child, but the rod of discipline will drive it far from him* (NIV). Daniel knew what to expect. I disciplined him, gave him lunch, a bath, and put him and Melanie down for their naps.

By the time I returned to the kitchen, the eggs had dried and hardened. I got to work with the scraper, mop, and bucket. I had been sitting there on the floor, working for about half an hour, when I realized what was happening. I was singing, praising God and having a really good time of fellowship with the Lord. Right in the midst of the mess! Like a flash, the Lord reminded me of that day a year earlier when my reaction had been so different. Glory to God, He had let me see how far He had brought me.

I soon found out, however, that He was not through with me yet. About a week later, I had Daniel and Melanie all dressed up to go out for lunch with a friend. We were about to leave when the phone rang. I answered it upstairs and found it to be a somewhat lengthy prayer request. Just as I hung up, Melanie's panicky voice called, "Mother, come quick, see what Daniel's doing!"

From the top of the stairs, I could see an empty syrup bottle and big white globs of something all over the carpet. In the kitchen, Daniel stood there calmly finger painting the back door. He was covered from head to toe with Crisco shortening. I think he was trying to make biscuits because after smearing three-quarters of the can all over the floor, cabinets, and himself, he had taken a five-pound sack of flour and shook it everywhere. Naturally, he was wearing his best clothes.

I stood there a moment, then burst into tears. I could not even reach him without falling flat in the slippery mess. An accusing voice whispered, "Where is your praise now?" Then I heard the Lord say, "I did not want to ruin your day with pride. Just let this show you how far we have to go." Then I felt the release and relief of laughter. I could really feel God minister His calmness.

My little Daniel, who often surprised me with a big kiss and "I love you, Mommy," sometimes exasperating but always lovable, was and is a joy to my life. Let me encourage you to expect the Lord to speak to you in the midst of the mess.

Chapter Six

Worship: The Pathway to Overcome Fear

For years, the Lord prodded us to have a regular family worship time. Each week, we made a new resolve in our hearts to be obedient, and each week we began again. A family worshipping together is a source of great spiritual power. That's why Satan, the enemy of our souls, tries in many ways to thwart our efforts. At the beginning of the day, caught in the hustle and bustle of activities, it is all too easy to think, "Let's put this off until later." Then when later comes, pressing needs always seem to arise to divert us.

On my refrigerator door is a card, on which is printed a very important part verse. *Whatever your task, work heartily, as serving the Lord and not men, knowing that from the Lord you will receive the inheritance as your reward; you are serving the Lord Christ* (Colossians 3:23-24, RSV). Worship should be a continual part of each day's activities and tasks.

As a handicapped mother of five active children, I stayed busy, and when two of them were preschoolers, my moments alone with God were rare. However, Melanie and Daniel enjoyed singing songs to Jesus with me as we did laundry, or dishes, or rode together. We openly asked Jesus to help us to find a lost toy or shoe, or to heal a skinned knee.   When the church prayer chain requests came in, there were three of us to agree together for the need. They learned by doing and by example, even as toddlers.

My older three children looked forward to me putting my arms around each of them and hearing me pray for Jesus to go with them to school each morning. Quite often one of them would mention a need like, "I need help with a test, please."

Do not forget the importance of asking God's blessing on your food. At our house, we took turns saying the blessing. Even the smaller children would sing a simple prayer blessing that I wrote for them.

Lest anyone misunderstand, please do not think I am saying that this should be a substitute for a regular, disciplined, personal devotional life. Instead, it should be an important addition to it. When children know, and they do, that their parents get up an hour earlier in the morning or stay up a while at night just to spend time with God in prayer, they have imparted to them more than what words alone could say about a relationship with Jesus.

Even though we practice making the Lord a part of every daily activity, there still needs to be definite time set aside and guarded jealously when the family can worship all together. We should not depend on the church to do it for us. It becomes a matter of priorities. I began to realize that we only have one chance with our children. We cannot go back and start all over again, as much as we might like to. Often good things can crowd out worship time. We never intend to, but the enemy of our souls is cunning.

We scheduled worship and family time after dinner at our house and labeled it top priority. We took the phone off the hook. By the way, even when we had guests, they seemed to enjoy joining us in this. *Train up a child in the way he should go, and when he is old he will not depart from it* (Proverbs 22:6, NKJV) I have been amazed at how God honored this simple obedience in our family. He has placed within our children a real eagerness and hunger to learn and given them an ability to memorize rapidly. It was the best time of our day.

First, we resolved to be regular and faithful to the time set. Secondly, we kept it brief, interesting, and stopped before we became tired. Thirdly, we tried to keep it informal. In our case, with toddlers, that part was the easiest. However, it should not be another play time. Finally, it must be varied. On some evenings, we read a chapter in the Bible, afterward discussing what we read. We would choose a verse to memorize from each chapter as we went along, storing God's word in our hearts. Other times, we would have a sword drill where each child tried to find a book or verse in the Bible first. Sometimes we would improvise a play, with each of us taking the role of a Biblical character. It was fun and often hilarious.

When our oldest child had the topic of evolution come up at school, our family time was spent searching for the firm foundation of truth for our children to stand upon. It is so important for us to plant in our children our Christian values. It is not the job of the school. The church can support parents, but should not be a substitute for them.

Music was a vital part of our worship. We would often gather around the piano to sing together. Even our youngest learned to sing in harmonies. In the Psalms, it says, *I have laid up thy word in my heart, that I might not sin against thee.* (Psalms 119:11, RSV). What better way to learn the scripture than to put a melody with it? Surely my cup ran over when I heard my little family singing Hallelujah together.

Deuteronomy sums up God's plan for family worship with these words. *And these words which I command you today shall be upon your heart; and you shall teach them diligently to your children, and shall talk of them when you sit in your house, and when you walk by the way, and when you lie down, and when you rise up* (Deuteronomy 6:6-7, RSV).

By teaching me to worship, God showed me the pathway to overcoming fear. From time spent in the "dark room" at Warm Springs to well into my adult years, I battled fear. After one particularly tormenting and exhausting battle, God began to show me that my victory had come through praise and worship. I saw that the enemy would supply me with fear continually as long as I focused on it. He is narcissistic and loved the attention I was giving to him. When I started to do battle in a different way, he left me. When fear attacked, I began to praise – out loud. I began to take every thought captive and recite scriptures of deliverance. I would start thanking God for His presence, His angels, His goodness, and letting my praise draw me deeper and deeper into a place of joy and of safety. Thank God I learned to change my focus.

Now, as adults, our children are all worshippers and are passing on to their children the secrets of how to handle adversity. We can worry or worship – choose to worship.

Chapter Seven

A Target

One of the definitions for the word target is *fired at*. Curiosity is a natural response to an obvious physical handicap. Most people are kind. Yet the people around whom I feel most vulnerable and unsafe are often religious people. It has never bothered me when curious children stare. I always want to engage them so they are not afraid to ask questions when their embarrassed mothers want to tell them to be quiet. I truly appreciate those who genuinely care.

I have had to fight the fears and insecurities that want to make me turn around and leave when I come into a new and unfamiliar crowd. It is difficult going into a strange place, especially a church where people believe in healing. It is there that most often I do not feel safe from those who want to tell me how to be healed when they have no relationship with me and know nothing of my history or walk with God. Yet, I am grateful for those loving friends who pray and believe with me and support me in my faith journey. No one could know the shame the enemy tries to make me feel. When I have to fight his lies in my mind about my appearance. God has been my Comforter, and I long to comfort those who hurt with the comfort I have been given.

It is wonderful to now be part of a church that believes in healing and all of the gifts of the Spirit without the condemnation or the weirdness found in many places.

I remember a time that vividly sticks out in my mind. "Did you know that if you had enough faith, God would heal you?" a smiling woman asked. I'm sure she meant well when she drove a knife into my heart with her question. She had no way of knowing the faith journey I have been on for much of my life. Since my disability is out there and very obvious to all, when I walk, or sometimes ride in my wheelchair, into a room, I often become a target.

My family always prayed and believed that God could and did heal. Indeed, in His mercy He had spared my life and healed me many times. When I was eight, I read the beautiful passages from scripture in Matthew and Mark in which Jesus healed the sick and spoke those words that encourage me, that if I have faith as small as mustard see, I would be healed. My childish faith cried out to believe it.

I went to my mother and read those passages to her and asked, "Did you know that it said this in the Bible?" Her heart must have been heavy as she heard me plead with her to agree with me in prayer. It sounded so simple to me. Just ask, don't doubt, believe, agree, and God would do the impossible. This began my journey into seeking to have the kind of faith that seemed to be required for healing. I must say that I came to a level of peace when I prayed the "If it be Thy will" prayer. Later, when I discovered that it is God's will to heal, I felt the burden descend on me again … somehow it must be my fault that God has not healed me.

I really don't remember much about the meeting I was attending that morning when the unsuspecting believer targeted me with her question. What I do remember is my time alone that afternoon in my hotel room. I was crying, in anguish on my face before the Lord, when I saw a picture in my mind. It was of me as a child, sitting in the lap of Jesus. I have since had a vision of myself dancing with the Lord, totally healed. I believe that it will be accomplished in my lifetime.

God has taught me that I cannot judge where a person is spiritually. Only God knows their journey and their heart. I am learning to not be wounded by what others say, since it still happens all the time. Recently, a lady approached me in the grocery store with the same question. I try to receive their love, to receive where they are in the Lord and ask God to help me not to judge them, but to love them. When I went back to the hotel room and got on my face before the Lord, I said, "God do you love me less than you love the other people who are receiving their miracles?" Her question made me doubt God's love. I did not know if He really, really loved me. I thought He had other favorites. Even though I had known Him for a long time and had known His favor, I was not sure that he loved me enough to give me a miracle. What He gave me was better. He gave me Himself, His closeness, the assurance of His love for me washing away the feelings of rejection and shame. He said, "I am going to use you just like you are! I am going to use you to touch other people, because when you touch people, they are not going to believe that it is you; they are going to know that it is all Me."

"Do you remember what they said to Me on the cross?" He continued. "'He saved others. Himself He cannot save.' You're tasting in the fellowship of my suffering."

I realize that shame is aligned closely with pride. The Word of God says that, *God resists the proud, but gives grace to the humble* (James 4:6, NKJV). It also tells us that if we will humble ourselves, He won't need to. I decided to turn the attack of the enemy into an occasion to embrace humility.

I am trying to learn to be thankful for the embarrassing moments in order to turn them into times when I can embrace humility, but I really do believe that God wants to heal and restore me. I am still standing on the promises in His word and remembering all the miraculous things He has already done for me and through me.

Perhaps the next time I am a target, it will be to hand me a key for my miracle. Maybe it will be the last prayer needed to those accumulating with my tears in the bowl in heaven. I welcome and am thankful for every prayer offered on my behalf. I am going to keep on praising my way through life and dancing in my dreams.

Chapter Eight

Thankful for My Journey

*M*y name, Ann, means *full of Grace,* and my life has been an opportunity for God's grace to be expressed. Without my handicap, I would never have been able to demonstrate what He could do for me. I would never have known how it was possible to raise five children, including one like Daniel, who was hard to keep up with without the grace of God in my life.

In 2 Corinthians, The Holy Spirit says, *My power works best in your weaknesses* (2 Corinthians 12:9, NLT). I have realized that my responses to testing can block my testimony from being used to express God's power. God has chiseled His command to forgive into my heart by giving me lots of opportunities to practice it. By not making a choice to forgive, despite the hurts we feel, we are making the choice to cultivate a root of bitterness.

Jesus commanded us to forgive seventy times seven. I believe that means every time we become aware of an offense, we are to forgive, even the offenses we feel we have already forgiven. Just do it again and again. Even while hanging on the cross, Jesus forgave, setting an example for us. Forgiveness is essential to having God's grace activated and expressed in my life. He has taught the lesson on forgiveness. I forgive, therefore I can be forgiven.

He has taught me how to be thankful in all circumstances and to praise my way out of tribulations and fear. He has taught me that resisting pride and shame will help me to draw near to Him and His grace.

During this journey, God has used my voice. I had the opportunity to go on a cruise and participate in a talent show while on the ship. I sang the song *You'll Never Walk Alone* and was asked to give a brief testimony.

What God did on that cruise was so beautiful. My new visibility became an open door to witness for Him. It allowed people the opportunity to approach me. There was a lady sitting at a nearby table and, although we had exchanged pleasantries, there was no real contact. After I was allowed to share a few words about myself, this same lady turned to me and said, "My husband had a stroke in 1987 and he has been in a coma every since then. Will you pray for him?" Then another lady said, "My daughter has scoliosis, and when she heard your testimony it brought new life to her. You will never know what it meant. She thought she would never have a full life, but when she heard you share, she thought that maybe there is hope for her." Another woman said, "My son was in a football accident last year. He is in a wheelchair. We don't know if he will ever walk again. Your testimony brought me so much hope."

I found myself saying to God, "Thank you for not healing me yet. See what You did! You touched all these people, and I would never have been able to do that had You already healed me." The healing on the inside of me has been greater than anything on the outside.

While reading as a young girl, I would imagine myself riding the black stallion. Later in life, I would imagine or daydream that I could run, or ride a bike, or roller skate, or water ski. But my favorite dream is that I can dance.

Chapter Nine

Brokenness

On June 18, 2008, Carter and I will have been married for 47 years. We are both well aware that the victories we have walked in are not the products of our own efforts. We have watched the Lord God perform miracles for us throughout our lives. We have been in full-time ministry for all of those 47 years. We started in Georgia, where we met and were married. Then we moved on to pioneer and plant churches that remain today in Indiana, Kentucky, and Texas.

We also pastored two Baptist churches while we were in seminary in Louisville, Kentucky. Additionally, we pastored in Denver, Colorado for over two years before returning to Texas in December 1990 to become the senior pastor of our church in Colleyville, Texas. Except for a short five-year period, we have always been senior pastors until now.

In the early summer of 2006, we contacted our friend, Pastor Mike Hayes, who helped us to transition into a new chapter of our lives. Let me share more of our journey.

On March 2, 1993, we received a call that our daughter Debbie, who lived in Washington D.C., was having her baby induced three weeks before her due date because of toxemia. Toxemia signals an incompatibility developing between mother and baby, possibly endangering both of their lives. We praise God that we arrived in D.C. in time to welcome Leon Carter Price II, our beautiful six-pound grandson. He was born at 2:00 in the morning on March 3, 1993.

That same afternoon, I was in the hospital room with Debbie while everyone else was resting from our short night. Quite suddenly, I slipped on something on the floor and fell on my right side, breaking my hip. Twelve hours later, I found myself in the surgical recovery room of the same hospital.

Against hospital policy, Carter was allowed to be with me for most of the six hours I remained in the recovery room, and God answered specific prayer there that I would not need a blood transfusion and that my blood pressure would come up so that I could be moved to a room. We were thankful to hear from the doctor that, although my bone was small, it was strong enough to attach a plate and pins to repair what resembled a crush more than a break. Carter and I spent the next several days in a private room where he was my loving, private duty nurse. He impressed the staff greatly. Then, and since my release from the hospital, my husband cared for me in ways no one wants to be cared for past infancy and made me believe he was glad to do so.

Breaking what we referred to as my relatively good leg presented unique problems for me. With the break to the right leg, I have had very little weight-bearing ability.

God truly used this time to show us the love of friends and family. We were so blessed by the wonderful support we received in ways too numerous to count. God's presence was very real and clear, and He has taught us much. My heart is full of love and gratitude. I am grateful that, though this was a season of stress in many ways, it was also a season of learning how to do warfare in the Spirit. I do thank God for the valley as well as for the mountains. I thank Him and praise Him for the trials He has brought me through, because as Andrae Crouch's song so adequately puts it, "If I'd never had a problem, I wouldn't know that He could solve it, and I'd never know what faith in God could do."

Despite the roadblocks which our enemy has thrown at us, Carter was a pillar of strength and an example of patience. He led our church through a season of change and renovation. He managed to do all with joy and enthusiasm while pastoring the church that he loves so much. The unselfish and self-sacrificing love that Carter demonstrates on a daily, and oftentimes throughout the night, basis truly reflected the same love Christ showed the Church when He gave up His life for it (Ephesians 5:25).

All five of my children and their mates blessed me and showered honor on me by putting their busy lives on hold to fly to Texas and give me the personal care I needed. We are all aware of the truth that it only takes a moment and one accident to completely alter our lives. Even though the Holy Spirit had been at work to prepare my heart, when the fire of testing and tribulation came, it surprised and totally inconvenienced me.

Then the unthinkable happened again. On March 27, 1999, I fell and broke my right knee in two places. Because of insurance issues, the emergency room sent me home with a temporary cast. The surgeon I saw the next week set my leg and put pins through my knee and a rod up the femur. Polio literature says that the longer pain goes unaddressed, the more difficult it is to bring under control. Thus, after many tries, I ended up with a strong, federally regulated drug for pain. It helped, though never fully took away the discomfort. It also slowed down my digestive processes so much that I had to take strong laxatives. I was still alive.

In August of that same year, I had a complete intestinal blockage and was hospitalized. Subsequent tests revealed a condition called Crohn's Disease. I have probably had it for years, but the pain medications and laxatives brought about a full-fledged attack. Crohn's affects everyone differently, but in my case I have two affected places, one in my upper intestine and another in the lower that would become inflamed and swell shut. I was hospitalized in 2000 during the month of May, again in August, and then a third time in October. Each time was a near death experience. In October, I received a blood transfusion. It was a serious and painful journey. After some new I-V treatments for Crohn's, I had a healthier November and December.

In May 2004, I had surgery in which 25 inches of my intestines were removed. Since then, I have had a steady improvement in my health. When the surgeon opened me up, he discovered that at some point between 1999 and 2004, my intestines had burst. He told Carter that it was horrible, that it had taken him two hours to chisel out the debris. Another miracle had occurred and God had saved my life again. My doctor had wanted to perform surgery in 1999, but I had resisted, believing God for a miracle. He had been faithful.

Many hospitalizations, blood transfusions, and other medical procedures effectively took me out of active duty. Carter has always been there as a wonderful support to me with the difficulties and limitations I have experienced. However, the new medical problems took a toll on him and the church, as well as on me. Carter was diagnosed with Parkinson's disease. All of our doctors have agreed that it was a stress-induced illness.

With concern for our church, people came forward with suggestions and solutions that produced some painful broken relationships in the process. When Pastor Mike became involved, he encouraged us to take a sabbatical rest for a few months because of our health issues, both physically and emotionally. We began trying to discover ways to become renewed and refreshed. We realized that even though we had lots of nice vacations, we could not remember a time when we had actually taken two weeks off in a row. Pastor Mike and the Covenant Church of Carrolton team came to help and strengthen us, and we have now completed a successful merger with them. Carter and I are now pastors on the staff of Churches in Covenant, where Pastors Mike and Kathy Hayes are the senior pastors and Pastors Ricky and Cyd Texada are the new campus pastors in Colleyville.

I suppose most mothers think that their children are the most beautiful, smart, and talented in the world, and I am no exception. Having said that, I know you will understand when I tell how proud I am of all of them. God has blessed Carter and me with His best. However, even if they were not my children, I would want them to be my friends. All five of them love and serve the Lord all over the country. They are each successful, married to Christians, and are training their children to love God. We now have sixteen grandchildren and counting.

My mother, Jimmie Richie, relocated from Georgia to Texas at the age of 80. She lives on her own, drives her car, and lives an active, happy lifestyle.

I have truly known the favor of the Lord.

Prayer

Our Father is so kind, loving, and good. We have so much for which to praise Him. We cannot do anything without Him. I ask the Lord to send His Holy Spirit to minister grace and forgiveness to the hearts of those who read these words. I pray that if there is any unforgiveness being harbored in our minds, He will help us to choose to forgive the ones who have offended us. We cannot change our emotions, but we can make a choice to forgive in obedience to His word. May He take away anything that would block us from feeling, knowing, and experiencing His love to its fullness.

May the Lord give us the heart of a worshipper, full of praise and thanksgiving. May we be able to say, "All things work together for good to those who love Him and are called according to His purpose." Amen.

About the Author

Ann Foster's remarkable testimony has made her a sought-after speaker. She has appeared on the 700 Club, TBN, and Daystar Television. She has also been a guest on *The Joni Show.*

She and her husband Carter have been in full-time ministry for 47 years and now serve on the staff at Covenant Church.

For further information, contact her at:
2836 Naples Drive
Hurst, Texas 76054
817.577.8263 or 817.354.5757
annf@charter.net